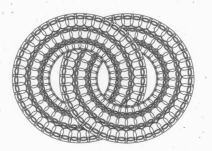

A Half-Life

A
Half-Life

David S. Cho

CAVANKERRY
PRESS

CavanKerry Press Ltd.
Fort Lee, New Jersey
www.cavankerrypress.org

Publisher's Cataloging-In-Publication Data
(Prepared by The Donohue Group, Inc.)
Names: Cho, David S., 1972- author.
Title: A half-life / David S. Cho.
Other Titles: Emerging voices series.
Description: First edition. | Fort Lee, New Jersey : CavanKerry Press, 2022.
Identifiers: ISBN 9781933880891
Subjects: LCSH: Korean Americans—Poetry. | Korean War,
    1950-1953—Poetry. | Vietnam War, 1961-1975—Poetry. | Roads—
    United States—Poetry. | Korean American poetry. | LCGFT: Poetry.
Classification: LCC PS3603.H59 H35 2022 | DDC 811/.6—dc23

Cover photo from the collection of Dong Ku Cho and Young Ja Yoon
Cover and interior text design by Ryan Scheife, Mayfly Design
First Edition 2022, Printed in the United States of America

CAVANKERRY
PRESS

Made possible by funds from the
New Jersey State Council on the Arts, a partner
agency of the National Endowment for the Arts.

CavanKerry Press is grateful for the support it receives
from the New Jersey State Council on the Arts.

In addition, CavanKerry Press gratefully acknowledges generous
emergency support received during the COVID-19 pandemic from
the following funders:

Community of Literary Magazines and Presses
New Jersey Arts and Culture Recovery Fund
New Jersey Council for the Humanities
New Jersey Economic Development Authority
Northern New Jersey Community Foundation
The Poetry Foundation
US Small Business Administration

Also by David S. Cho

Song of Our Songs (2010)

Night Sessions (2011)

Lost in Transnation: Alternative Narrative, National, and Historical Visions of the Korean American Subject in Select 20th-Century Korean American Novels (2017)

To the living memories of:

The Cho, Yoon, and Lee clans . . .

Family, friends, mentors, and communities who have
supported me, my family, this book, and other
projects . . .

The long history of US Asian immigrants, migrants, and
Asian Americans, their long-standing presence,
influence, and work . . .

The power of American Ethnic Studies, Asian American
Studies, and their long-standing presence, influence,
and work . . .

The power of the Civil Rights era and activists, then and
now, their long-standing presence, influence, and
work, in whose legacy we live . . .

Those in this country, and across the globe . . .

Those here, and those dearly departed . . .

Those on this side of heaven, and on the other
side in glory . . .

Please accept this work as an offering of
my appreciation—

I am deeply indebted.

Contents

III. Journeys of a Hyphen

I.

Sovereign Asymmetries

A Circle of Fragments

Today in Seattle,
it does not rain—
I wish to kiss my son hello.

———

The stomach of cashew nuts
smooth and curved, banana-like,
once opened, the color of light dirt.

———

Radiating orbs of light,
blue skies dark as the ocean,
my bathed baby son, my contacts, sink-drained.

———

Oh glasses,
your two-dimensional view,
seeing less of the world so strangely pleases me.

———

Oh circle of sharp edges,
oh, fragmentated length of you, keys,
your push, my pull, causes me to circle you, round and
        around you again.

Existential Poem no. 1

I lean against a chair,
arms hung low, expecting gravity
to be suspended, a push

exerting back
to fill the air,
which would otherwise

be nothing,
and find none.
It's a contemporary creation,

a design friend of mine would say,
that the curved arms
of this chair

exist for a reason,
that even the surrounding space
of the head, the arms,

one's hips, that its
form follows function,
like the slender bow

of reeds in the wind,
or the curved contour
of a shirt-hid shoulder,

breath held
like an open book's
pages fluttering

before its closing.
Breath that does not
want its release

because it is sweet air
exhaled like one's
cloudy exhalation of smoke,

its cigarette-rough sweetness savored
on a gray day. Those shoulders,
my friend says, are leveled

into the arms
not unlike a young man's
wound muscle, down

to his knotted fist and fingers,
collapsed into the thick seams,
its curled length

bringing into presence
an idea
of its own design.

Existential Poem no. 2

Can sound transgress
from the mouth of a crying
baby to the deaf ears

of a father's deep slumber?
Does a physicist consider
wavelengths, its particle matter

shooting through the walls of air,
sound? Is the muted silence of
such deafness truly "dumb"?

Can a father fear the death
of his son, when that son
has not yet come into existence?

And upon that moment when a son
gazes into the face of his progenitor,
can a son fear for his father's life,

before even understanding the meaning
of his own, like a peony's bud
blossoming into fullness, a poem

in the mind of poet? Today
I hold the face of my son,
whose death I fear

will someday floor me,
whose wrinkled brow
bears to light

our likeness,
whose eyes direct-gaze
stare at me like my father's,

his thinning gait
looking more like a young boy's.
Today I hold the face of my son.

Two hands square on his cheeks,
he kisses me, lips apart
as if to suck the marrow

from my cheek,
as if to say *hello*,
for the first and last time.

Existential Poem no. 3

The grumble and creak
    moans of wood in the house

       when all are asleep.
    The clicking of claws

       in a pail we used
to store the just-caught crab.

          Front-window sun shadows
fall through the air, gridded,

       beam-dust suspended within,
    suddenly stopping at the back door.

The skeletal shells of the crabs
    we have just eaten, odd pail-noises

       we still hear.
    The quandary of knocking

       on my bathroom door
    to get my son out—he's locked in—

Open the door, we say,
    Turn the knob, it's easy . . .

       The slow gyration of the handle
         stopping—not knowing what else to do,

     responding to our door-knock,
he knocks back.

Gravity's Pull

Where my son will be
twenty years from now,
who can tell?

Today I watch him
at a birthday party—
sushi, California rolls,
sandwiches, and smoked salmon.

Yes, this is a party of doctors,
mostly Korean Americans—
which also means

heaping plates of *sangchu*, red lettuce,
beef *kalbi*, *bulgogi*, spicy pork,
the smell of *kim chi*

floating with the balloons,
held above the other kids,
the rented, hot-air, bouncing inflatable,

he is screaming in delight,
round the other children,
around me, my wife,

screaming with no one
around, the vibrations
of the plastic his only sight,

his breath, the hot air
pumped in, this rubber castle
pulsating smaller then larger—

all he seems to need
for company. Why in this moment
my heart swells

like one engorged helium sphere
I see rising against gravity's pull,
yet tethered to the chair,

this sunken feeling
of another balloon floating away,
nearly, but not quite.

Spring in Seattle

In half-closed shades,
of vain wishes to let in the morning
warm, yet still cool, I know

A door in my bedroom exists
because its darkness remains
in long squares, longer than the morning light

A seagull's cry from the canal
pierces miles of absent
gray turning to pastel light

Shells cracking,
evergreen seeds growing ready
to leave their nestle

A dark blue and black
blanket, checkered, surround my children,
nestled within, the friction

Sparks that leap
in the still yet
night light.

Lullaby

Today the desire to sing
some song to my son
strikes me,

forcing me to consider
songs that my father
had uttered to me

as a young boy—
trying forever to grow
and catch this figure

of a man
who is walking down
the street so far away

a shadowy man-form—
an outline really—
wondering *is this my father?*

or some stranger
of similar stock
squared shoulders and legs.

Today I consider the question
of whether to sing
to my son,

remind him of my own stocky body,
the flesh-form, in part,
of his own blood and form,

and remember that
the only song my father
ever sang to me

was his whistle—
a deep draw of air,
let loose

through his grooved tongue
on teeth, his cheeks puffing
into his dimples and jawline,

then out, like note sounds
from a young boy on a recorder,
a young boy blowing

through a blade of grass,
a tired melody that brings joy
to his son, the upturned

angles of his face, curving into
a weary half-smile,
as if to say,

chama—"endure . . . hold on"—
that same smile I see on my son
who looks at me

through the square frame
of a photo
on my desk.

II.

Poems for Harry

A Young Boy's Life

1.

Harry Kim awakens, hears
what might be the cooing of birds
in the early morning half-light
yet dark, runs down the hallway

to see his father kneeled before
a chair as a pastor would
before an altar or pew.
He is praying, Harry discovers,

in a tongue that seems to come
from the heavens, or at least
the rafter of pigeons above.
And in silent reverence,

which equals love for his father,
Harry imitates that strange roll
and garble of unintelligibles
in his mind and later through

his own lips. He practices them,
imagining their original meaning,
the moment now a meditation of sorts.
A young child whose brows knit

together in a furrow, closing out
time, he listens to the curtains unfold,
smelling the dust gathering
in rays through the open window slits.

2.

When Mr. Kim was a boy,
Harry's age, he grew up fearing
for his life. The threat of spies from the North,

the constant pang of hunger,
his family always digging under the house
for somewhere to lie

when the siren warned
of bombs. But even through all this,
Sung Min's father would awake

in the early morning,
pray for his country,
for his family,

and weep until blood
poured from his sweat,
pleading for the survival of both.

One day, his father
claimed there was a train
going South,

away from the waves
of Northern armies.
He would send them all

to his sister's, finding a way
down to them.
This was the Lord's will,

he would say. *Listen for when
the fighting stops,
and I will be there.*

Sung Min would listen to the radio,
hoping to hear about the war
stopping, his father arriving,

ready to meet him
early in the morning
to pray together,

kowtowed, loud,
and no one to hear but God,
and the church walls around them.

Sung Min would arise
and listen to the radio,
hearing only the static speeches

of the great war hero,
General MacArthur,
the shrill sirens,

and rush of wind
that came through
where the trains used to.

3.

Harry's father catches the young child
at dinner curling his lips as if to whistle,
pausing to ask his wife

whether young Harry is now speaking Korean
or English, and how he must be her son,
not his, that is trained to speak neither.

They observe the young child
thinking he may be disabled in some way
to be so happily occupied with the noise

of what could be a train, or a vacuum, or the wind
washing itself in circles on the window,
or the tree branches grinding against the house.

The father palm-claps for Harry to stop, worried
that the child so preoccupied would fall
out a window, short-ropes the window

open and shut halfway, gently rubs his child's ears in
to not protrude out like batwings, brushes his hair
to the right until the follicles follow.

To know this kind of love,
you must see the father ask Harry to bring water,
mul jom juh, mul jum caju walrah,

and the pleasure it brings them both
when Harry promptly stretches his body
to draw tap water in the cup, and bring it.

Such a love, Harry, tired of a day's work,
would request the same of his son.
Young Harry promised himself

to awaken earlier, meditate harder,
intone more correctly
his father's roll of the tongue,

bringing not a palm, but a psalm of praise,
a blessing of hands
over the son's small head.

4.

One day, Harry and his father go out
to plant a tree. *Why,* Harry's father explains,
whenever you look out
this window, you must be reminded

to grow steadfast, straight, silent as a sapling,
solid as the ring's growing core.
When I was a young boy,
everyone wanted to grow up

to be like the great General MacArthur.
But not I. I wanted to grow up like Harry S. Truman,
born on a farm, gone to war, come back a hero,
senator, then vice-president

through FDR's failing health,
president of the United States,
winning his second term over Dewey,
the impossible made possible—

only the Lord could have willed it.
One problem though—my name,
Sung Min Kim.
Would "Give 'Em Hell—Kim Sung Min" work?

What to do but bear a son,
name him Harry S. "A True-man"
preaching the good news, a salve
to souls, helping faiths
as small as mustard seeds

move mountains.
Bury me here, so I will lie
next to you, watching
to see you grow sturdy as this tree.

To this, Harry nods his head,
watching the leaves swirl around
the roots reaching out, thirstily,
in the light autumn rain.

5.

Harry never saw his parents
hold hands, let alone

kiss, as sometimes the parents
of the neighborhood kids would,

coming home before dinner.
But Harry would see his parents

sitting inches away
from one another.

Mrs. Kim would roll sesame-oiled rice,
spinach, yellow pickled radish, and long

pieces of meat into a bamboo mat,
pressing the roll tight.

Mr. Kim would watch
eyes half-opened, as if to sleep—

how he loved to see the rolls sliced vertically,
the white, yellow, and black slivers separating.

Cut clean through the core, precise
as the rhythm of her "Amens"

uttered between the pauses
of her pastor and husband's prayer.

The slices, black
as a lacquer plate

hanging on their wall.
Two silver men eating

from a pearl pot of rice,
the moon shining like a nickel,

savored in the mouth
of a man who would work all night,

come home, watch his wife,
like a potter,

take disparate items
and roll them together again.

6.

To know what happiness is,
go to the church that Mr. Kim
started from scratch: an old school,

bought with the mortgage on his house,
repaired with his own hands, and begun
with only a congregation of three—pastor,

wife, and child. Go to the Busse Woods picnic
they have every year, when all the Koreans come out
promising to attend every week after this.

Watch them relax their tired legs on the straw mats,
fan themselves from the heat of the summer,
refreshed by the smell of rice, slender, long mackerel,

gongchi, on the grill, marinated meat and *kim chi* for lunch.
See the people gather to brag about their children—
their honor rolls, the new piano and violin

prodigies of the century. They'll gorge on the gossip,
fill their bellies, take a nap, then the games begin.
One will pull out a soccer ball, and the men

become boys, who push one another for the ball,
tuck in their guts, stretch out their stubby legs,
and run as if the family's honor

like some prize in heaven were awaiting,
running like the days when they served in the army,
three years given for the love of their country,

never knowing how difficult it would be to work
as an immigrant in the US, when in the '70s,
the sting of Nam and Pearl Harbor

brought them hard looks from their bosses
and fellow workers. For three hours, they forget
all this, content to knock one another over,

hear their children and wives laugh,
let the sun lobster their skin,
for as long as it still remained day.

7.

after Philip Levine

To know what work is,
watch Harry, a young boy

of age nine, burn his thumb
on the pot of water, check if it has boiled

enough to place a few beef franks in it,
boil them red, broth forming from the fat

and beef in its long sacks.
Watch Harry put the red hots and their soup

in his father's thermos, pack a smaller thermos of coffee,
and a bag of rice, chanting to go with his father,

help him clean the spit, gum, and mud of the kids he played
with at school, wash the windows clean, and make

what Harry's friends made black with their bowels and
        bladders,
porcelain white clear.

Watch Harry leave for school
as his father comes in from the third shift,

go to his study, pray for a while, letting his hands
straighten from the mop's hold, his hair dry out

from the sweat and ammonia—his mind cleaning out as he
        prayed
to his God for sweet rest, strength for the next night,

and many thanks for the money to take care of his family.
See his fingers callous over the years

and turn dark from the lack of oxygen.
See him stay up to study and prepare for the next

Sunday's message.
Watch Harry's eyes gleam when his father,

bagged eyes and all,
tells Harry that he drank down the food,

rice, meat, soup, and all—it was good—
for it was made by his only son,

and that Harry must study hard,
prepare for the unexpected turns in life,

work hard as his father,
for, before the Lord,

that is what work is.

Growing Up Harry: Harry's Junior High Linguistic Lessons

1.

Because Harry was lonely,
moving to the white house
and sidewalked

suburbs
and needing
to get out

and make some friends,
he went to the park, where
kids would BMX-jump

on a hill, all evening long
until it grew too dark
for even the buzzing bulb lights.

Invariably, one would say
fuck you and Harry would blink
and not understand—

was it, *you,*
fuck you-
rself

or *I—*
will fuck
you.

Harry, still a boy,
believed that
babies came from his mother's stomach,

not lower. And in either case
of his interpretation
or their proposition, Harry preferred neither

and would say, *No.*
They would laugh
so mouth open wide,

one's teeth shined
yellow like the bulbs,
the other's shined white

as the cement and stars
that night.

2.

What could Harry do
but team up with boys
at church, take off after

the last "Amens," watch
the Chicago Cubs. Here a stocky white man
would field the unwieldy baseball

with "eyes" at short, backflip
the ball to his taller, slender,
Jewish teammate at second, skipping

over the cleat-first sliding baserunner,
the ball emerging out the cloud of dust
to his African American first baseman. *This is America,*

Harry thought. A game that actually embraces
all colors, including the Cubbie blue,
green ivy, and brown dirt, dirt that soiled
their crisp summer-white home uniforms.

They would practice
this Bowa-Sandberg-Durham
double play until dark, fielding

the ball crisply, catching it on the rise
with their cow leather mitts,
feeling the ball

in the dark well
of their gloves then their palms,
carved out

by the swift grab of the stitches
leaving the hand, two-fingered,
the index like a gun's barrel and tip.

3.

Harry and his boys would watch
the neighborhood boys' fathers

hit grounders and fungoes, catcher's mitts pounding
by their sons' pitches until dinner.

Homework done, dinner, and two hours of light
to spare, the Korean boys' fathers went to work

for their night shifts, and so did the boys,
playing against dim lit school walls, empty fields,

until their eyes twitched, the nerves
firing into their muscles

for a short hopper to their left, a crazy divot
bouncer to the right,

practicing, hoping for a chance
to play the neighborhood boys.

Even while walking home,
they would catch the night bugs afterwards,

pretending the taillight glow
was a grounder in the hole—

the corner of their eyes,
muscles twitching

at the only night light
they had.

4.

What Harry thought of girls back then
was nothing different than being interested
in the odd shapes of women:

why the bell-shaped bottoms, unlike
the flat ones of his friends? Breasts more full
and pointed than most boys they knew,

and ladies' pants—*why the zipper?*
Why the oversized gold frame glasses,
Chia-Pet-like pile of black curled hair

on older Korean women, as short as he?
At a Korean supermarket with his mother,
Harry suddenly stopped agape

to see his mother's friend,
full breasted, sweater pulled high
on the right, letting her milk loose into

the mouth of her son. Harry ran down the aisle,
cheeks flush-red, knocking over stocked cans of mackerel,
both moms smiling at his sheepishness.

Poor Harry kept looking on, as if
this was a circus, a small window
he could insert a quarter,

hear Jack Palance's rough voice
on Ripley's TV show, calling into reality
the bizarre, asking for him to "Believe It or Not!"

5.

Harry went home one night, depressed,
wondering when chance would let him
meet the neighborhood boys,

wondering whether next time
they said, *Fuck you,* or *Go fuck yourself,*
he should say, *Yes, fuck me,* or *Yes, I will fuck myself.*

No, to this invitation, he resolved—he would not.
He could not. *How was this even biologically possible?*
Later, one of the BMX boys'

mothers pulled him aside,
accosting him for causing her son
to come home so late

with a mouth so foul,
sewer water
would be too clean.

It made him smile,
the possibilities of the moment,
the poetic convergence,

like Karma,
a school lesson learned,
coming around full circle—

fuck you, he muttered under his breath.

6.

One day, Harry walked down the street,
a Korean man staring intently, for quite some time.

Harry checked his zipper,
patted his hair, straightened his shirt,

concluding no Korean traditions were violated,
nothing to be stared at, but the customary glare

one Korean gives another
to see if they knew that person,

their family, or some common friend,
in some way.

Harry did not.
The man did.

The stranger approached him,
asking, *Are you Kim Har-rhee?*

Son of Kim Sung Min?
I am, Harry replied.

The man broke down into tears,
sobbing, *My how you've grown,*

telling Harry
that he named his church

after Harry's father.
Harry walked to that church,

stared through the sunrays of dust
sat in its long walnut-covered pews,

marveling at what the silent work
and death of one man could build

in the heart
of the next.

Harry concluded that a martyr's life
was a life

that could not hope
for such a title,

until dead,
like his father.

Thinking—
he too would like to be a martyr

someday, but how to hope
for such a title

that itself is dedicated
to having no desire

of the world,
to faith and service? That

what he desired
was to have no desire?

So complicated a calling,
he decided,

is to live like one—
not letting anyone know.

The Edge

for Steve Chang

To know Mr. Smith, you have to know
that in the '70s, he would travel around,
marvel at the excitement

of America's secret white flour, cocaine,
but would never join in. Marvel, that to some,
"dope" was a funny joke, to others

good journalism, and to most,
something to be enjoyed,
like a cigarette from another world—

or at least, one that would take you there.
Smoke a joint maybe,
drink past the midnight hour

definitely, but never past the point
of passing out. To lose that moment
of alert wakefulness, even in times

of peace, was to lose his edge. Even
more so after the Korean
and Vietnam Wars. *The edge,*

he would tell Harry and his kids,
*is like the time
I went to a bar in Texas,*

*saw a lovely Latina sitting alone—such beauty
matched with such loneliness, was like a lost
wallet of money suddenly found—like that parable*

from Jesus himself. Why not sit in silence together?
Or speak with broken-English sighs, or let whatever
may come between us arise like the moon

and stars together? Her English was fine,
and so fine was our conversation
her boyfriend came and asked me

to step outside for a lesson, that
he would teach me a thing or two.

No, tank yu, *I said in my best*
broken Konglish, and he began
making like a train, smoke billowing

from the top of his head and ears,
dark things coming from his
smokestack of lips. He asked me

to step outside again. I said,
I speekee no Ing eu rish, no Americanesee . . .
Then in perfect American English,

I growled, So take it easy, dude, *people laughing*
so hard, it sounded more like wolves howling
at the moon, which brought only

more heat from his head,
more smoke, and dark things from his mouth,
like a stove top, and told him

if I had a skillet, I could have made a meal,
fried fish or an egg, on his head. He made a fist,
and I made bad, laughing at the insolence

of his youth—in Korea, in a split second
I would have slapped him, flipped over a table,
my friends holding me back.

But here in America, and he so much bigger than me,
he hit me, and hit me again. His friends pulling
out metal knuckles, rocks, pipes, anything outside

or under their coats, all hitting me, me groaning
with laughter, them stopping
when seeing their fleshy abdomens

in the corner of my eyes, I back-kicked like a mule,
front-kicked like an American football punter, side-kicked
like a ballerina. No more laughing. No more chatter. Music no
    longer. Only heads

getting hotter, more dark things from their mouths, fists,
shoes, hitting me until a hot sweetness,
black like liquor, filled my back,

my spine, the bitterness filling my mouth.
The police even came, used batons.
Even then, I kicked past

beyond my hour of consciousness,
like your father, who prays with such passion,
after and before a long day of work, crying

as if to ask for the dead to come alive,
as if to ask that his own life could be taken,
as if another poor soul would instead be blessed.

I kicked swiftly at the pin-sized image
of their bodies from the side of my eyes.
Yes, those puny eyes they were screaming

about. If you don't believe me, check it out
in the newspapers. They locked me away
until I remembered my last name again.

It took years. But I am here.
It keeps me awake, when at night
I need to fight off the sleep.

And when sleeping, I remember, and arise,
though the day is yet dark to me and the world.
I arise to take back those years lost to me.

I arise to the moon, greet
the dawning sun, to be here,
and laugh about it with you.

Harry's *Playboys*

1.

Harry's ears blossomed open
to a chorus of teens yelling,

Open your eyes!
Happy Birthday!

To this Harry replied cautiously,
My eyes are open.

Oh, they replied.

2.

Silence,
Harry learned
at that moment, was

when the saliva spiral
sounds
from a dog's

hungry jowls
could be heard
even in a clubhouse

of thirteen teens
breathing heavy
with confusion.

3.

It's all right, Harry—just do like us!
they said.

So Harry did.
What Harry saw filled him with shame,

because he had never seen women
unclothed, naked, white, black, swollen in areas

as if to burst, sitting lap wide open.
What filled Harry with shame

all the more,
was the swollen longing in Harry's blue jeans,

his heart becoming
filled with a desire

for women unlike
anything he had seen before,

who most shamefully
were his "boys of summer,"

who sat cross-legged
unashamed. Harry was

overcome,
with his first look—

second—and third too.

4.

Harry walked away
not wanting to burst

the birthday surprise
of their longing.

Hae-rhee, his uncle tried to explain,
this is natural, *dis nateural,*

I hab sum doo. That Harry found
in the bathroom closet

was true.
True as his uncle grunting,

the right arm tattoo
locking together,

apart, together,
while finishing his push-ups.

That these magazines,
these meetings,

makes your pepper grow
into more a man every day.

The heavy breathing
of his uncle's dog

slack jaw open,
snapping closed,

open . . .

Cheers for Harry

1. A Strange Thing

A strange thing for a foreigner's son
to see a crowd, one by one, stand and yell,

arms raised, only to sit, and the next stand—
"a wave," they called it.

Stranger for the crowd to see
three Asian boys, Walter Hong at shortstop, Harry Kim at second,

John Chi at first,
skin dark as the dirt, get down, scoop up

the red-seamed baseball, toss, throw, and catch,
3-4-5, into a double play

instinctively, as if they ate
all their meals together,

as if they slept together
in a cramped room,

talking only of baseball,
practicing every inch

of every possible day—
"Hip, hip, hooray, Ho, Kim, Chi, double play."

Like an unholy American trinity
of three "yellow" boys,

now brown,
making tough plays in the hole

routine, the ball slung around
the infield.

2. From the Bleachers

Whoa, Ho! Great Play!

> *Hip, Hip, Hooray . . . Ho-Kim-Chi Double Play*

Ho's got hands like money . . .
  Cha-Ching!

On a fly ball—fly them all outta here . . .
       You mean fry them outta here . . .

Isn't that the Chinese restaurant owner's kid?
      Yeah, he sits in the back, frying egg rolls.
      That's him—he sits back there on a high chair rolling egg,
         rolling like a king.
             How about this one—good zing, my Egg Roll King.
              Watch this play! That's my ERK!

Another Ho-Chi-Minh Double Play.
    Play like you're back in the jungle!

He runs like a Chinese helicopter.

           Chi, did you see that hit?
       Anyone see Kim Chi as dark as that?

              Don't look at my Ho that way . . .
          That ain't no ordinary five-dollar Ho!
                Don't you be callin' my boys ho-chies.
         Ho ain't short for honey on my team.

   Ho-mama.

Damn, that sure is one Harry—Kim!

3. The Walk Home

For the first time in his life,
what was to be a blessing,

a name destined for greatness,
great as his father, pioneer pastor,

great as the "Give 'em Hell, Harry"
Truman, former US president—

great as it was
to hear the crowd roaring,

it was not enough
to stop Harry from cursing his name,

his own kind,
and white people who laughed

anywhere around him,
his heart turning black as dirt

under the pale moonlight
dull as a cadaver.

The Locker Room

1.

It is a secret thing, though it does not seem a secret
to Harry. He and other Asian boys
he meets do not do like other boys do

in the locker room. Some men, with their
washboard-taut bodies, walk around naked
as the Greek David, and as long and full

in places where no leaf could cover.
Others have bellies that sag,
with penises that sag all the more

like overripe fruit on a tree whose
skin is rotting off, everything out like laundry
to dry, but far be it for the boys to stare,

though they do in silence. There are men
as small as twin pods hanging from a leaf,
and others full as a curved plantain.

But the men's fortune, or misfortune, does not help.
Should the Asian boys walk around bravado as others?
What if they are not macho enough in size

to cavalier their parts that so many brag of?
Jokes, where most boys laugh, but Harry
and the other boys, Asian, blink to understand,

listen in silence, imitate, and join
in the laughs of the many. So here they stand
in a high school locker room, sliding

their shorts off, wondering, if, how,
and how long to shower naked as the others,
washing their privates with soap,

lathering themselves clean,
the white foam sliding off their skin
like pubescent male charge.

2.

In Korea, Harry recalled all men—boys,
men, and the elderly—would go to a public
bathhouse, sit in the steamed

water, then in the ice-cold water;
after a day of doing both,
all were pruned loose, relaxed, and small,

wet buddhas sitting in meditation. But in America,
Harry's friend, Shin Huk, thought the shower etiquette
the same, and while showering, let loose

his bladder, the yellow liquid spilling on the floor
washed away by the soap and water into the drainpipe.
But this was not the Far East. The boys here

thought this was far out, and started to squeal in delight
and horror, pointing to Shin, *Shit, Shin, why'd you do that?*
Shin, shit—it's OK—go ahead and do that too! as if he were filthy

like a pig, leaving his entrails out for all to see—perhaps later
he would eat from his own excrement. Harry stayed quiet,
wishing it would all get over, knowing

his family could have done the same. But Harry
had not. He observed, taking a mental note
to talk with Shin after, vowing never to do the same.

Harry wetted a towel, wiped himself off,
slid on his shorts,
called it a day, and went home silently.

In the background, the howls of laughter
and steam slid through the narrow
cracks of the door opening and shutting.

53

The Ballerina

The girl was dressed in tights—
everything she wore in fact was tight.
Tight enough that her breasts seemed

swollen under the tight press
of the gown, her hair kept
in a bun, stretching her face

thin, the heavy powder
making her face pale
as the dead.

Harry watched in fascination
as every leap, curve, and dance
came alive

with the music
and changing array of colors
behind her.

Standing on her toes,
leaping from them, pirouetting,
her small dress creating circles

in the dark, brought whispers
of excitement from the audience,
Harry too. There Harry found himself

swept in her moves,
her pale face, emotionless,
her mind, like an engine, whirring

a few steps ahead,
whose mind had to focus
out the next day's criticism

or applause, whose mind
had to deliver to the next
run of strings or boom

of the low drums,
whose mind pictured
the moves of the teacher

before her.
There in the half-circle
aisle that sat silent,

Harry pitied the ballerina,
for such a doomed life
of pleasing others,

yet found himself
weeping into the open circle
of his sleeve,

the people clucking
like hens
at this commotion.

After the Concert

Harry went home that night,
turned on the same adagio of strings
he heard earlier,

the music speaking to him
words that were not there,
just as Harry's memory

of his father was there,
faded, yet knowing his father
would be pleased with Harry's

growing love
for the run and blend
of violin harmony.

The ballerina's
pale outline went round
as the record

on the stereo's
revolving platform,
a moment when to Harry

words became
a dark ink seeping
into the pores

of the blank page,
a prayer of sorts,
a meditation and occasion

to write down.
About this, Harry knew,
his father would be displeased,

a word wasted
in something that could have been,
instead, a night of cold labor

silence,
and a morning given in words
of prayer.

Harry Meets His Father

In his sleep, Harry's ears alert
to a growing rumbling

from the ceiling, like chains,
middle seam of the ceiling swelling

as if to burst, coming undone,
tooth by drywall tooth.

Harry stares intently
at the zipper, the ceiling to fall in

like the bottom crack of an aquarium,
the water breaking through,

and sees the face, unmistakable in form:
pug-nosed, hair parted to the right,

square faced, bony high cheekbones,
Harry asking, *Who are you?*

This pale-faced pastor sighs,
hand patting his hair, replying,

Who do you say that I am?

And before Harry can answer,
before he can cry out *Appa*

or "father" in Korean, this ghost
of a man, this apparition of thought,

leaves through the cracks,
becomes lost in them,

the zipper closing done,
disappearing,

leaving Harry with only
questions he has searched

all his life for
and now found, come to him,

but with no evidence
but himself, his dreams,

an open window, a ceiling
painted hospital-hall white,

silence, and a cold bed
to account for all his miseries.

Praise for Prozac: Notes from Harry's Journal

To see Harry, look through
his bedroom square window,
frames of his mother, father,

his cousins, and their awards
wrapped on the walls
all around him, meditating

on how to join them
like stars in the sky,
their constellation

of fame, wood-framed
around him, like the night sky
above, to which

Harry watches TV,
watching incessantly,
the only voice speaking to him,

besides the cicadas
chirping in the trees,
the mist rising

from the damp earth.
Harry's deep breath,
the only reply.

———

Today, I am reseeding the bald patches of my lawn

———

These days I feel like I can't live with myself.

Neither can my hair.

It's begun to fall out, piling up in the four corners of my earth:

>   To the North, a tangled mess by the
>   northeast mattress corner by my head,

>   To the West, a spider web of hair on the handle of the
>   fridge,

>   To the East, a small pile under the
>   T-trap of my bathroom sink,

>   To the South, an edge of carpet-like hair on the
>   left side of my TV.

———

I once wrote:

>   "For no reason
>   I dream of hair,
>   it whispers old memories.

>   How terrible it falls—
>   it feels like rain
>   drop by drop,

>   leaving me bald.
>   My friend had
>   hair black as a bushel

>   on the fertile soil
>   of his head.
>   Memory of him too

feels like rain
            running away.
   Sitting and lying I listen

with an emptied mind.
            I don't need hair,
   I don't need rain."

_____

After watching 12 hours of cable TV,
      I realize,
            I don't need hair
      I don't need rain
            I don't even need my mind

                        Sy Sperling and your
                        1-800-HAIR-CLUB, why
                        don't you leave me alone?

_____

I don't want people to leave me alone.

But when you are alone, you have no one to say this to.

My mother once said that to be alone is a virtue.

I must be quite a virtuous man.

But I feel dirty as a beggar.

A beggar who shuns the coins of the rich for pride,
      a beggar who does not believe in charity,
      a beggar whose pride lets him live in filth.

A filth he is not proud of.

———

I met an Asian beggar in college town, tried wiping up the table,
    set him some food to fill his skinny-lipped mouth.

I felt akin—he had long whiskers, like a catfished version of
    my good friend, Kai.

Fuck off, is all he said.
    Fuck me, I thought. I heard he was a professor.

I am now studying to be a professor.

———

Why I do not talk in class, I do not know.

Perhaps it has something to do with the way I was raised.
Perhaps it has something to do with how much I love my
    father and mother,
            something to do with that to me reverence and
                submission is love,
            something to do with my cousins whom I love
                like my siblings,
            something to do with those cousins who are
                all doctors,
            something to do with being a poet, and
                begging for the scraps of my muse, my
                imagination,
            something to do with my literary peers going
                for a beer, smoking a drag, going to the
                coffee store, talking about Kafka or their
                cats.

Perhaps something to do with those days—I go to church,

And on some days, I feel the poetic rhythm of the hymns sung
   by the Korean parents, their bodies swaying like prairie
   grass in the wind,

And on some days, I feel the tempo of drums, the pittering of
   children's feet running wild in the sanctuary, basement,
   their hands grazing and hitting the stairwell rails, anywhere
   but in the sanctuary, their parents' hushed whispers like
   bass beats punctuating the silence of the walls,

On some days, the noise of ladles on lids, making the Sunday
   gook—no, not a swear word or euphemism for Asians—
   good, tasty *gook*—Korean soup—ginger, rice, beef or
   fish broth wafting through the floors, like the hushed
   conversations of mothers, grandmothers, aunts, rising
   up like incense to the sky of the basement ceiling,

And on those days, I do feel like an insider. But it's a bit of a
   trap.

I'm an outsider looking in—I didn't grow up in Seoul, I grew
   up here in the States,
      and wary of being so alone in school all the time,
      and wary of when my peers are so polite to me,
      and wary of when they are not—

Will I always have to live like a performer or a bum—the
   muse of everyone's fascination?

Or will I always have to say "yes-yes" in deferential silence,
   like a caged ape who is applauded when following
   directions?

And is this why I'm supposed to be good at math, spelling,
    computer programming, piano, Ping-Pong, pool, anything
    with rote memorization, and routine practice until the
    late hours of the night?

Or perhaps it is because my people tell me
        to be the insider pulling the others in.

I'm in up to my head in both worlds,

Can I observe both and still get in?

    ——

I hate people passing by and saying hi out of courtesy.

I hate it when they do not do even that.

I hate it because Asians will stare at me, staring as if they
    know me, without a greeting.

I love to see an African American man tip his hat or give a
    slight nod to respect his brother.

I've heard this too is a dying thing.

When I tip my hat to my Asian brothers, they think I'm posing
    as an Afro-Asian, a chocolate-covered Twinkie,
and the Black brothers think I'm a yellow Uncle Tom.

My name is Harry and my family in Korea thinks I'm a white
    covering on a yellow soul—*come back home*, they say, like
    I'm an egg peeled back to its yellow yolk.

Or they think I've grown bone white in my heart, and become
    a twinkie.

And when I try to act like a solid-colored piece of *dackgwon*,
   yellow squash,

I can't stand myself—it's a color of the flag I wasn't born
   under

And a color I have been trying all my life to understand.

I'm tired of trying.

I'm tired of talking—tired of having to say it in a poem.

I'll be quiet.

Perhaps, I've been too quiet all too long.

I'll sit and think about that to myself.

———

When I was young, I wanted to play football. Couldn't, so I
   played piano instead.

I played piano for eight years until I saw the *Time* magazine
   article on the "Asian Whiz Kids." They all played piano or
   violin—I was nothing special.

My cousins played both.

I chose to play clarinet instead and let the small wood rod
   make noise from my puckered lips.

Please do not read this as code for my need for oral sex here.
   Freud died many years ago.

Enough of the puckering.

Then my friends and I played baseball. Coaches put us
in positions where our short stubby legs, refusing to
surrender, could do no damage: right field, second base,
catcher if no one else would, places where I watched the
dandelions grow big as my head, the dirt growing into
dust, trying not to squint at the batter's swing, and the
pitcher's squeeze of the ball.

The league made us a package deal. One draft pick "for them
all."

Hip, Hip, Hooray . . . Ho-Kim-Chi Double Play.

———

I was sent to Korea because my uncle wanted me to find my
roots.

Geun abu ji, oldest father, my dad's oldest brother, pulled out
our Korean genealogy, told me where my spot was, like a
prebought plot at a cemetery.

After five minutes of passing pleasantries and chitchat in
Korean, taxi drivers started yelling at me for forgetting
the mother tongue and love of my "home" country.

Was enrolled at a government program for high school
Koreans in the West, saw young Korean Americans
mostly, Korean Australians, Korean Germans, Koreans
from all over the globe falling in love, flipping head
over heels for each other, flipping tables over, throwing
watermelon rinds, chairs, and fists, chunks of hair
grabbed by the fistful from heads, all over who fell in love
with whom, and stole whom from whom.

A beefy Korean Minnesotan making like "Macho Man" Randy
    Savage, all sunglassed, long-haired, ripped shirt, and
    popped arm-veins bulging at his flex, cowboy hat—the
    whole bit—raspily asking us to "snap into a Slim Jim,"
    selling his dad's store beef jerky from his suitcase for
    ten times the price in Korean won because we wanted
    American meat so bad at camp.

The price of it all—oh, how we belonged—and not—all at
    once.

America, stop showing me movies, historical moments, and
    news clippings about the Korean War, the development
    of Korea in the South, the containment of communism in
    the North, and how lucky we Korean Americans are for
    America saving us from both.

Stop telling me about the Whiz Kids and the Model Minority,
    as if you cut our hands, out would come the DNA of
    our blood: a double-helixed chain of piano and violin
    notes, the elements of the periodic chart, a stethoscope,
    tongue depressor, and rubber reflex mallet, saying yes
    to everything, no to nothing, or not saying anything at all,
    but working double—triple—hard.

Someone, tell me about Korean America. Someone tell us
    about Koreans in the cane fields of Hawaii, the henequen
    fields of the Yucatán; Korean American novelists
    Younghill Kang and Richard E. Kim, about East Goes West
    and Lost Names; about Olympic diver and gold winner
    Sammy Lee.

Someone tell us about Mary Paik Lee and Ronyoung Kim,
    who detailed the lives of women surviving Korea's
    colonization and migrating to America; about A Quiet
    Odyssey and Clay Walls; about Korean emigrant women

surviving a civil war tearing apart a country still divided;
about carrying nation, a child, and a few belongings on
their backs; about America's new "gooks" who officially
had no home of their own as global colonial subjects
giving birth to a new generation of Americans while
working two impossible jobs and setting up a store of
their own, making dimes out of pennies; about the use of
Korean "comfort women" for the Japanese military.

Someone tell us about the Willows Korean Aviation School
to train for anticolonialism abroad; about Lieutenant
Young Oak Kim fighting with the Japanese American
100th Infantry Battalion, and later, the 442nd Regimental
Combat Team in World War II, to "go for broke," a "double
victory" against fascism abroad and racism at home,
retiring as a colonel; about countless Korean immigrants
to the East and West Coasts, the Midwest and South,
whose Korean American heartland stories we may never
hear, but all know, and live.

Someone tell us, like the Black brothers and sisters, why
we aren't learning or taught about our history and
achievements, a beautiful linguistic mix of Korean,
English, and a mixed-fused Konglish, literature and
movies—forgive me for borrowing from Black language
and culture, but why ain't we got no movie like *Roots*?
Why ain't we got even a TV show like *Sanford and Son*?

———

I came back and tried to pick up football again.

My hands would not move, couldn't get it.

What I did get:
Kim, isn't that like Smith in English?

Didn't you play violin
before this?

God damn, your parents must have hated you, to name you
like that.

Kim, God damn it, you can't finger the
ball like a violin!

America, I don't want my way. I just want a piece of your
apple, and you can have a piece of my black bean pie. Can
you do that for a Korean American brother?

———

I once was proud of myself for having spent a semester to
myself to write;
I devoted this time to a book of poems, itself devoted to my
parents.

To this, a peer said, "It may enlarge your vision to write on
topics outside of your family."

Well thank you.

Here's a poem not about my father,

but about Gerald Stern and his poem on the airy sadness of
empty shirts, Jewish American history re-collected like
the pages of Art Spiegelman's *Maus*,

about Gwendolyn Brooks who says *we real cool* in the funk
tone depths of jazz,

and about the women of my department noting the
insufferable wrongs in US women's history, ripping apart

70

the he-man words like (he)r)men)eu(tics) and the worlds
of "his" "story,"

and the LGBTQ crowds in America, crying LesBiGay for
suffering done to them,

and for Asian Americans who were given nothing more than a
silent *Aiiieeeee!!!* in movies—

for men in Hawaii forced to mail order picture brides,
for women having to marry men they never knew, becoming
his servant, a plantation owner's indentured laborer, an
indentured servant's servant—all this to live in America—

for the Japanese American men roaming the hills of Europe,
facing hard looks, expected to yell *Kamikazeee!!!* and
become a human bomb, these lone Asian American
soldiers serving in the Second World War, opening the
fence doors of German concentration camps, imprisoned
Jews walking out and away, their parents and friends
living in the "internment camps" back home—

This is a poem not about my father,
who polished away the days as a janitor,
cleaning the shit, piss, and spit of my friends that even
their parents would not clean,
refusing to move so that he would have enough money to
start a church for fellow Koreans,
polishing the floors until Saturday night, to deliver a
message with *chung*, fellowship divine,
preaching that Sunday on the Sermon on the Mount—
*blessed are the poor in spirit . . . for they shall inherit
the earth—*
which, if true, in heaven, my father should be given at
least a continent,
going back to work on Monday.

There is not enough to say. There is too much to say.

There should be more.

This is not a poem about my father.

It's about more than my father.

It's about pleasing my dead father,

A live desire.

But who would notice? Who will read these poems?

So I stay silent.

All this silence is killing me.

Which I don't understand—

If I am dead already,

Why so much head-noise?

Or if I am alive,

Why all this silence?

———

Dear God,

I hear the chirping of cicadas.

I'm still waiting for my call to
    become a pastor,
        like my father, and his father
            before him.

72

In the heavenly fire of who you are,

All I hear is

Silence.

———

There are days I feel like I can't live with myself.

And the other days, I don't want to.

I'd rather see myself die.

I'm quiet about it because it is depressing.

I'm quiet about it because I'm depressed.

I'm quiet about it because my father would be depressed.

I'll take some Prozac.

It's made me even quieter.

Everyone, just leave me alone, and let me suffer

In a pit of failed promises.

It's what you've done before anyhow.

———

III

Journeys of a Hyphen

A Love Poem for My Wife

Today the wind blows. It is Chicago. And it is cold.
So cold, the wind has streaked the clouds
into puddled blues, still with resolve—or so it seems.

So resolved, the sun tries
to set itself lower on the horizon—
lower in Chicago means

dropping beneath the line
of cement, steel, sand,
and lake water.

The cemented gray of exhaust
on snow, salt-ridden tires,
highways covering the city

like a maze—cars scurrying like mice.
And back to the subject,
I do not know why

I do not write love poems
to my wife.
A question asked of me

when plain faces turn quizzical,
an opening of the eye,
a circling twitch of the lips.

I do not know why
I do not write love poems
to my wife.

Today it snows in Chicago—
the wind carries the flurry of flakes off the lake,
the wind so brusque, it carries itself off the frozen lake,

the snow suddenly stopping.
It is windy in Chicago.
Today, I wish a love poem for my wife

would arise, like this broken-windowed,
three-storied, red brick building.
Arise from a field of long-dead

Chicago grass, yellowed, the whispers
of wheat and prairie grass in its heads,
holding the promise of spring.

This building set atop this field,
set atop timber, steel, and cut stone cylinders,
in this muddy marsh, this great layer of jelly,

this Chicago cake of clay, water, and gravel.
A love poem for my wife that would rise
like the sun over Lake Michigan,

a red hazy blanket. Like the sun setting,
a dark crown over this field,
this building, this Second City,

this city of impossible contradiction,
this city of two seasons—winter and construction—
this city whose fall season is too short

yet too golden, burnt orange, and brown leaf fall glorious,
this city of animals—the Bears, Cubs, Bulls—and apparel, the
    White Sox,

this city of hard work, harder vowels, consonants, and sharp
    syllables—

you can hear in the mellifluous staccato of its heroes—Mike
    Ditka, Dick Butkus, Walter Payton,
you can hear in the rattling barrage of the *El*, the elevated
    train, crisscrossing the city,
you see the red lights, this scarlet pair of eyes, fading in the
    distance, wheel-sparks on the steel tracks,

creating its own heat, creating its own swooshing wind,
the winter gale off the Lake, creating a swirl of snow,
this Windy City of my birth, this *city of broad shoulders*,

for this Korean American woman I so love—
finally,
a love poem.

The Apology

My father asks the illogical and I have no answer—
how a man on *Real TV*, a Minnesotan, has a fancy
for fur, picks up his 12-gauge shotgun, and heads north.

He has a name for men like these, this Twin-Cities
man who decides to pheromone his camouflage
like cologne, and like Thoreau, head for the woods,

the mountain forest dissolving his smell. That is
until the deer solved the smell, sniff-ramming
that man—no, not a doe, not smart, and not having

much fancy for fur from then on. He says that men
with such common sense, or rather such scent,
are from the south, islands where in Korea, men

do eat dogs for soup, tell time by the bird and season.
Winter-locked in homes, wives locked to their men,
they drink rice wine and tea to shiver out the cold. Summer

drains the wind, brings the rain, families straw together hats,
lines furrowing in their foreheads, dig rows, work before
the sun rises, wondering if the morning dew

is not their sweat. And through all this talk—the deer
the hunter attacked, the farmer whose back
breaks like straw in the heat—my father talks of work.

How though we are born an ocean and war apart, work
is like a rose in bloom, making a face hot and swollen,
everywhere a rose to pick. How once, the lips of a machine

pressed down on my mother's arm, deftly, as if it fit,
leaving her head, my father's, and brother's, three springs
of water. Just a young man—a boy really—what could be said?

I, like the deer, will wander the neighborhood north,
go by scent, a bone to pick, hungry
and wanting to eat that rose, thistle and all.

Entropy

1.

There is a deer
lying by the road. No
make that a half-deer,

half of its fur
swaying like the flowers
and prairie grass

by the side of its head,
moved by the interrupted
sunshine and air

which is not air,
but wind. Wind created
by the internal combustion

of gasoline passing through metal,
passing through a large, chambered engine,
meeting a small flame. Yes,

the engine's dish,
her skin so yellow,
so red hot,

his pistons are firing, his plugs
sparking, his sparks plugging
away, his finger-long digits

exploding into fire. Oh look at her,
so red hot on the outside, some say,
her core is white cold.

Some say, when they meet,
it's true combustion, love at first sight,
others say consumption,

subsummation, titillation.
Whatever the word, there is heat,
there is noise, there is consumption,

consummation, this terrible odor,
which some experts say is an addiction,
people standing up to the muffler, sniffing,

sniffling, warmed, touched by heat,
in a long Chicago winter.
Somebody tell me—if a metal engine,

gas, and fire are ignited,
is this a mechanical *ménage à trois*?
Is the exhaust gas

a car's fart? And if so,
can a car's flagellation
be called a product of love?

I don't know. Ask the deer
by the side of the road. Who,
like me, is half there

and half not,
like the whistling wind
interrupting the silence.

2.

How do you explain this
half-deer, half there,
and half rotted away,

gone, as if mind and matter
could somehow dissipate
into this car moment of silence,

window half down, wind oscillating
through, ears adjusting to the pressure,
up and down, like the sound of road signs,

cars coming, here, and gone. This silence
existing for just long enough
for the fumes to blow by like perpetual,

hiccupped broke-wind, for my balding tires
to carry away just a piece
of deer meat with,

for this crow that spots its open flesh,
for the ants that look like legged, black sesame seeds,
gnawing at this treasure-mountain of meat,

carrying tiny orbs of bone, a white trophy
on their backs, returning home
to their mound, to their maker, family,

dinner for all. For this sun-bleached grass, yellowing
during the day, and with winter coming,
yellow grass which floats across

my window, for just a moment—
my eyes, white toward its core,
a two-fold radial center

of blackened brown,
its corners like a flame's
outer edges—red.

Chicago Highway Poems

1. Lake Shore Drive

Here on Lake Shore Drive
you can eat curry buffet on the Devon exit,
no meat for $2.95, see the pawn
elephant jewelry shops,

and on Belmont, see the Oyver Roman Gift Shop
proclaim, "tenemos telefónicas tarjetas
para vender" and sell clothes on the side.

Go to Lawrence, hear the karaoke bass
blast, smell the seasoned fried legs of chicken,
meat dumplings, and buy a pizza: sausage,
cheese, and fermented ripe cabbage
kim chi for spice on its top.

To know what happiness is, go to Hyde Park
where the Latinos lay down their shirts,
let out their hair, let their Spanglish flow,
and play soccer.

To know sadness, visit Wrigley Field
and be me for one day
in just this: I love the Cubs.
Ballpark of green ivy, nectar of Bud-
weiser, the official
gut filler of the North Siders.

We are the "Kings of Beers,"
to love a team who melted down,
second to the Mets in '69,
choking on the Chicago heat, humidity,

and most probably, a red hot—*hawt dawg*—
of the '45 World Series. Cubs fans,
There's always next year.

The proverbial underachievers.
The lovable losers. We know
the heartache of Harry Caray,
who died before the Bryant-, Báez-, Rizzo-,
and Epstein-led 2016 World Series championship—
Harry, may you now rest in peace.

To know sorrow, stand by me
at a Dempster Street funeral where a mother
of my friend stops breathing

from her sobbing, becomes a Korean coiled *z*,
all knees and shoulders heaving
on the ground as her

son's casket is lowered. She wants
to follow him to the grave, but
the father stops her.
He is as pale as a ghost,
and the hymn is not yet over.

"Welcome to Chicago,"
the billboard over O'Hare, I-90, 94,
says. Thank you.

This autumn, this is Chicago,
this is home.

2. 94 East

Chicago is crowned like a prince. If you don't believe me, see
the skyscraper domes and climb the Sears Tower, watch
Lake Michigan labor to wind out the smog of chimneys,
furnaces, exhaust pipes, millions of them like stems on
fruit, and see the fog roll in from the North and settle in
over the city like silver-gray velvet on a crown.

Chicago is the Windy City.

Chicago is not an apple. Chicago is meat. Chicago is the
Sinclair-made-famous city that ripped the hides off
swine, bovine, slicing buttocks for ham, sternums
cracked, chests laid rib-open bare like the nautical bones
of a ship hung vertical, packed its Stock Yard trains, and
unpacked them with dirt-cheap immigrant labors whose
hands became pink from the cold air. Their own hands
becoming leather.

Chicago is a city of broken noses. Listen to one say *hawt
dawg, da Boolls, da Bears, Da Coach, Dick Butkus, Mike
Ditka*, the Chicago beloved whose iron fist once shattered,
hitting an equipment locker, saying after, *Let's win one, for
Lefty*. Hooray.

This is Chicago.

I once asked "Johnny," who wanted to work for my father, if he
had a green card. He smiled and said, *No, but I could get
one*. I never asked again.

Johnny worked two jobs, one for my father, another holed in a
factory, bought a home, got married, had three kids, sent

money back home to family, hoping to someday return as
the prodigal son-gone-American come home.

Billboards higher than the crosses say, "When It Rains It
Pours"—Morton Salt, you are right. You are always
right. In the summer, when it rains, it pours all heat and
humidity in Chicago, like a curse from God—listen to the
oscillating cries of locusts in the trees.

But wait until the winter. When it snows, lips under a wool
hat freeze, chap, stiffen, curse the Lord Almighty. Car
windows crack and spread like a spider's web, kids warm
themselves by the muffler like an old potbelly stove,
parents shoveling snow and ice for a week with a spade
and shovel, laying salt. When it snows, it pours.

Chicago is not ashamed.

Chicago is a city "that works." A city once burned to ashes
by the hoof of an overmilked cow; riddled by Capone
bullet mobbings and prohibited beer, riots in 1919; raised
up highways in the '50s, road lights everywhere like old
gas lights; built skyscrapers whose antennas touch the
clouds in the '70s; saw the '80s horizon of homes shake
from the O'Hare Boeing plane thunder.

The Kennedy. Eisenhower. The Dan Ryan. Driving these
highways gives you hope like a cross: Vatican, Greek
Orthodox, Episcopalian, First United Methodist. Crosses
that stick out like chimneys. Crosses that stick out like a
mother—Holy Church of the Virgin Mary—where a Holy
Father can lead you to repentance.

Chicago keeps its business in the family. See the guts of a
father, his hot dog store bought when Old Man Daley was
still mayor, arrive at dawn, work the grill with his sons,

go home at dawn, balding, bellies all full of meat. Richard
M. Daley, the old man's son, became mayor too.

Have it your way, says Ray Kroc of the McDonald's Co. on a
billboard over I-94.

Chicago will. It always will.

3. I-90

Over the "Skyway"
highway from Chicago to Indiana, it looks as if it will storm.

Over Gary, Indiana, the black clouds look like it will always
    rain and thunder.

You can hear it through the hum of rainwater on the electric
    cable towers
that line the side of the road like Good Friday crosses.
    Crucified towers.

Crucified cross towers. Dark Jesuses. Towering Jesi.

Chimneys of steel-producing factories, erected high like
    construction sets
we played with as kids, spitting black clouds out into the sky.

But these are not toys.

These are jumbo Erector sets "not for those under 18,"
for those who dare.

As I drive by in the dark mornings, I see young teens walk
    through the doors
with showered-clean heads, white teeth laughing,
and swear that by dusk, they've become dirt-head,
    ash-smeared adults,
whose sweat pours off like steam,
wobble-kneed, walking to their cars,
smoke pouring out of their own chimneyed cigarettes.

Then the night shift begins.

Sweltering labor of steel welded to steel, girder to girder;
red light of the torches making their own fire,
the workers gasping for air.

This is no child's game. They are playing with fire.

They are smoking.

They are producing man-sized exhalations and giganto
    Bunsen-burner
fires, the carbon monoxide and sulfur fumes becoming their
    own clouds.

These are nights stretched long that never see the light of day.

God is in neither the clouds by day, nor the chimneys that
    make a pillar of fire by night.

Gary, Indiana is Gotham City.

Holy smokes! Someone, send out a signal and call the Batman.

Someone, send out a 24-hour, 365-day storm watch for the
    people.

It may rain, but I swear it never storms. The clouds just look
    like they will.

Indiana Highway Poems

1. I-65

A black cartoon crow
on the billboard over I-65
says that "There is more

than corn in Indiana."
That black bird
must be crazy.

This is Indiana. Where the sun sits
in the sky like a fiery marble
roasting the husks of Indiana corn,

turning the grass straw into hay.
Here the hair of Hoosiers
all seems blonded by the sun,

their faith turned on like a TV
where you can get only CBS
and two channels of 24-hour

prayer lines, the slaying of people
by the spirit, faith healing, and
worship that makes you want to jump.

There is no room for even Elvis here.
Basketball here is King. Legends
are made on the court, where

they wait to see
pint-size Davids from pea-sized towns,
face Goliath schools that enroll thousands.

Basketball here flies like revival.
French Lick's Larry Bird, his proboscis, and uncanny shot,
is crucified under Bob Knight, Bloomington, IU, transfers,

resurrects in Terre Haute, for the ISU Sycamores,
and comes back as the Messiah-Coach of the Pacers.
Hallelujah! Here in a New Life Bookstore shelf

sits on the left, a book on knowing Jesus,
in the middle, a book on loving God
and praying in the Spirit,

and on the right hand, sits *Hoosier Hysteria:*
Indiana High School Basketball. Hallelujah—
Amen! Here phone calls at the market

are a quarter. Here you can catch
the latest news in the library
with the *New York Times* or its

younger left shelf brother,
the *National Enquirer*, for those
inquiring Hoosier minds.

Here a man can own a
hundred acres and for years
keep time locked

with his name on that land,
his sideburns long, and his top
cropped short.

He can watch the news,
the NBA on TNT, on his farm,
with his field of corn,

with his name on the door, on satellite TV.
Amen, Amen, Hallelujah—
Amen.

2. Route 231

When I first arrived,
I thought the place was to be
like the Kansas fields,

wild grass growing
high as the waist,
in open wide plains of dirt,

Ma-and-Pa grocery stores
selling cold soda, scissors, spools of thread
for under a dollar; a Ford pick-up by the roadside.

But this is not Kansas. Be aware.
Here in Lafayette,
I've seen Confederate flags sold at gas stations,

farmers machine-sickling their acres of corn before the winter,
piling the cobs high in silos.
Silos that stick out like the twin breasts in Song of Solomon.
    Here

in Lafayette, the farmer may only own nine sheep and a few
    cows,
with a Daihatsu tractor, an acre of corn, a two-story,
    central-air, heated,
red brick house with satellite TV, a Ford pick-up,

a Toyota Camry for travel.
Ma and Pa do not run a one-story, independent grocery store,
    flat-house convenient store,
but greet and manage a one-story, one-block, half-mile wide
    store that sells everything

you want to target: BB guns, bubble gum,
digital antennas, better-than-leather NBA basketballs,
Spalding footballs, bibles, soda by the gross and more.

It's as if good old Sam Walton gave back to the good old boys
from Indiana and had his Walmarts spring up like grass seed
on every major street, a percentage of the profits going to the
    schools.

3. Lafayette, Indiana

Indiana is a state of first names you can call on.
You can hear it: *Good old Sam. Hi Hon. Hey Pops.*
Every Hoosier home has a Pops.

He is the Godfather of Hoosiers.
The Don. The elderly neighbor.
The store owner.

Pops. I met him while trying to play football for a day, semipro.
Pops pulled out a pair of spandex stretch nylon pants with holes
for pads to fit and shoes for me to wear.

Pops played the last decade at defensive end, knocking the
     heads
of sassy kids half his age,
and was put out of commission at age 55.

His last knee surgery.
Pops had to lay his pads aside and
don his post office-blue government uniform full-time.

He is now a coach.
If anyone misses a block, he runs in, screams to be *let at 'em*.
Everyone snickers. God bless Pops.

God bless football.
If God were to live in Indiana,
his name would be Pops.

He'd have two first names,
like the ones I've seen on mailboxes, postcards to Mary Jo,
John Johns, Wade Earl, Bill, and Verna.

Jesus Christ,
I think I've seen Boss Hogg in a car.
His name is Scott Niles, player's coach of the Lafayette Lions.
     Scott is loyal.

Scott is a patriot.
His shorts commemorate his two brothers who were Army
     Rangers,
a brother for each leg

he's had three surgeries on, and still plays.
See the skull and cross of bones on
the black shorts

on each leg.
Scott is a soldier of death on the field.
Scott is a family man.

He has two of them.
His divorced wife's kid plays football, and is coached
under Jack Jackson, aka "Action Jackson,"

who I taught in class,
which makes me a Hoosier godfather by instruction
and cow-leather football.

The Hyphen

I am a flickering flame's wick.

A wicker basket's weaving line, seen and unseen.

I am the bastard child between a dash and nothing,
the interrupted lines of a road.

An elongated period, a blot stretched long,
a cat whisker, nose hair, eyebrow plucked,

floating, tossed midair, tweezed

by two parabolic lines, hung together
by a metal-wishboned hip,

itself hung together between
the thumb and index finger,

the trigger, a pointed
digitus secondus.

I have a friend named "Hyung,"
an age-old Korean name

for older brother,
who, upon immigration,

his fifth-grade teacher
pronounced "hung,"

baptizing him
a new creation,

without water, without the Spirit,
without even a dove,

reborn to a life of questions
on his endowment, biological

measurements, peeks at the urinal, countless
chalkboard games of four-lettered hangman.

I am a sidewise comma with no bend,
an exclamation point turned horizontal,

a blip of ink filling the pores
of a blank page, period-dropped.

A blip of space, bandwidth of light,
ones and zeroes—off—

then on—visual code seen—unseen,
flash of light

infilling the screen
like cyberspace rain.

The line of what was,
and what is, like

an "Asian-American"—
all that excitement, silence—

the pain, sorrow, and joy.
A halved dash,

the line between two worlds,

I am.

Notes

"A Love Poem for My Wife"

"Second City" is a common term for Chicago, often thought of as the second largest city to New York historically, but due more to the city's second rising after the Great Fire of 1871.

The phrase "this city of hard work" refers to Mayor Richard J. Daley's Chicago slogan, "The City That Works," denoting the city's blue-collar roots and "hard work"-work ethic.

"Indiana Highway Poems: 1. I-65"

This biblical-like basketball narrative is presented in the movie *Hoosiers*.

Acknowledgments

Many thanks to the editors of the journals and magazines where many of these poems first appeared, sometimes in different form:

Many Mountains Moving: "A Young Boy's Life 1 (*Harry Kim awakens, hears*)," "A Young Boy's Life 5 (*Harry never saw his parents*)," "A Young Boy's Life 7 (*To know what work is,*)"

Spoon River Poetry Review: "After the Concert," "The Ballerina," "The Locker Room 1 and 2"

Portions of the second part of this manuscript, "After the Concert," "The Ballerina," "The Locker Room 1 and 2," "A Young Boy's Life 1 (*Harry Kim awakens, hears*), "A Young Boy's Life 5" (*Harry never saw his parents*), "A Young Boy's Life 6 (*To know what happiness is,*), and "A Young Boy's Life 7" (*To know what work is,*), were originally published in *Night Sessions* by CavanKerry Press, 2011.

Many thanks to my family of five, my Cho extended family, and the many families, communities, and people who have supported, nurtured, and inspired this book all over the US and globe. Here, I would also like to thank the CavanKerry staff, who believed in this work, for their tireless efforts: Joan Cusack Handler, Gabriel Cleveland, Dimitri Reyes, Joy Arbor, and so many more.

CavanKerry's Mission

A not-for-profit literary press serving art and community, CavanKerry is committed to expanding the reach of poetry and other fine literature to a general readership by publishing works that explore the emotional and psychological landscapes of everyday life, and to bringing that art to the underserved where they live, work, and receive services.

Other Books in the Emerging Voices Series

A Half-Life has been set in DIN, a sans-serif typeface in the industrial or "grotesque" style. It was designed in 1995 by Albert-Jan Pool. DIN is an acronym for Deutsches Institut für Normung (German Institute of Standardization). It was published by FontShop in its FontFont library of typefaces.